THE SORROWFUL LIFE OF A YOUNG BOY

FIDAL SURENDRAN

Contents

Contents

Contents

1. Keyli

She was the one who,
Makes me smile.
Even though we were separated by miles.
She made my fears go away,
In a way nobody couldn't.
Too far away for my hands to hold,
And too near for my heart to Love.

Looking at her face,
I came to know,
She was the one,
Who can wipe my agony.

For the first time in years,
I fell in love with a girl,
Who can't speak my language.
One who was miles away.
But yet she was the one,
Who brought light to my heart,
And smile to my lips.
For me,
Love is not just being with someone.
It's feeling someone,
Even if miles separates.

And you are worth every miles between us.

A girl who lives in the other side,
Made my misery fade.
When i was on the edge of death.
with those pills in my hand.

I never wanted to run behind good faces.
And i don't have any more energy to catch good hearts.
Yet i found a person.
Who was full of light.

Where i couldn't withstand a fight,
With my heart and felled in love.
Fate took a dramatic turn,
Which burned,
Every bit of suffering,
And made my heart blossom again.

You showed me sunshine,
When i only saw darkness,
You made me smile,
When i only felt pain.

You'll always be on my mind,
And forever in my heart.

I will love you forever.
As long as i breathe.

FIDAL SURENDRAN

My love for you is and will be the strongest Feeling inside me.

2. Anxiety

Trapped by anxiety.
To only see endless fear.
To only feel endless pain.
Even the smallest thing,
Made him afraid.
Constantly mind speaking to him.
About every bad possibility.
He argued with his mind.
To just be kind,
To him sometimes.
But he didn't knew,
Anxiety was a devil.
That only gaved him pain.
And can only give him pain.
To escape,
He has to find his own light,
But he couldn't.
Drowned himself in meds.
But that only got it worse.
For his pain and fear,
There was no cure.
he considered himself,
As the god's unwanted child.

3. FIDA: a poetry mixed with emotions

On the nights of hot summer,
Saw a girl with a dark hair.
I knew that it would one day rue,
Knew the danger, yet towards I walked.
After all I would be a fool not to notice the way,
The sunshine plays,
With her hair.
She was a cocktail of emotions
Even I can't write my name without passing through hers
She showed me a light of hope,
Holding to that every day I woke
But she left without a word,
For years, from her I never heard.
Not even a single word.
Deep down for her the place I gave her in my heart stayed the same,
Years passed was so many
But she never came.

4. Curse

A boy born as a curse.
Born on this earth by dark force.
Surviving from all painful things.
He began to search for the source.
But never found any.
He asks himself,
Why am I like this.
Why am I the only one around here like this.
Anger was emerging.
Tears was falling.
Wanting to end this misery,
But he couldn't.

5. Missing

Her memories aren't leaving,
From heaven her hands are waving.
But what can I do?
God didn't tell.
From hell I started to yell
What can I do?
She couldn't hear
All those pain how can I bear?

6. Eternal love

There is nothing in the universe as you,
But the moments I got with is few.
You made a fence of happiness around me.
But now there's no we.
maybe we'll never meet again .
But still can walk through hell and heaven like parallel lines
To infinity and beyond.

7. Light & Darkness

Light and darkness felled in love.
Never been together,
Never holded hands.
But yet they were in love.

Their love was so strong.
She was bright as a full moon.
He was like an eclipse.
A feeling felt by both,
A feeling as beautiful as,
A garden filled with flowers.
But where there is Light,
There will be no darkness.
That was the curse given to their love.
Curse that can never be broken.

8. Loitering has no end

Infornt of the gates gates of heaven i linger.
But i couldn't lay a finger,
On her.
Waited for years.
Hoping to be yours
But that was a world,
Which was walled.

Our separation was betide.
But i wanted to be on her side.
The day of her cessation, Started all.
We were in god's thrall.

I was alone gloomy, but still loitering.
I can hear her sing.
But her, i couldn't see.
For that i plea.

9. No more left

With ear plugs on,
Hearing the songs.
Mind wants to cry.
But there were no tears,
left in me.

Smiling outside.
Shouting inside.
Standing in rain.
To hide all those pain.

All these years,
Every single day,
Trying to find you.
But I couldn't.
God hid you in a only place
Where i couldn't enter.
Waiting outside the gates,
Covered by clouds.
Begging.
Only for a moment.
Only for a minute.
But the tears were Unanswered.

10. Dark covered days

Seeing the dark covered eyes,
Which never saw sleep.
I'm In drugs, They thought.
Nobody knew how hard i fought.
The time the sun wents down,
Their starts the lonliness.
Their starts the fight.
Nobody saw that sight.
And called him an addict.

11. Magical Highlight That: Portrays Hope

When the situation got worsen,
Accidently, to my life came a person.
And brought a tiny bit of light,
To my darkest fright.
She was easy to like,
Because she was just like me.
Her personality was contagious,
And anxiety was outrageous.
A person that people write hope poems about,
Without a doubt.
With lots of darkness inside,
Still her eyes shine like sun outside.
A beautiful soul lost in this world,
Which was so cold,
To unfold hope.
I know so many last words,
But I'll never know hers.
Born as an angel,
Who was made of light and hope,
She could brighten the darkness,
With a single smile.
Had a light of her own,

Which was shown,
To all, in the form of hope.
One who believed in magic.

• 14 •

12. Hope

On the edge of life.
Thinking about jumping.
Hearing so much loud noises inside my head.
And the loudest was,
Just die.
Just die.
Die ....
An easy way to cure this pain.
There's nothing you can gain.
From living like this.

Standing on the point,
To end this misery.
Then came a person.
A face i never saw in person.
But the voice,
It made me think about hope.
Person who said this too shall pass.
The urge of death pauses,
For a minute.
More words made it a possible thing.
To that i'm holding.
To death i say,
I'll survive.

Not just this day.
But i'll survive each passing day.

13. No escape

Night without sleep.
Constantly hearing a beep.
Not going away even by covering my ears.
Maybe it's because of my fears.
Every night seeing the same face.
Every night seeing the same place.
Running from my mind.
But every time I look behind,
It's still there.

14. Unbearable curse

Everyone thought living was great.
Nobody knew we are cursed.
God cursed us with feeling.
And the most painful was love.

The curse i hate.
Changed my fate.
Used me as a bait,
Pushed me from the heights.
To the world of pain.
To the world of suffering.
To the world of the cursed.
Burying me there.
A place way too far,
From everyone.
In a lonely place,
Covered with every moments of pain.

15. Art of agony

Art of agony, He paint.
Can't hold it, i'll faint.
To meet, We were disallowed.
That's fate, he Avowed
Finally i know.
But not accepting it though.
He gives my heart a shake,
And said, Coming here was a mistake.
Feelings i had was queer.
But i never knew the death, it was near.
It's now been a year.
Still has no loss of fear.
God said that was fate's Sate.
Saying there will be no end to my Hate,
Towards him.

16. Past miracle

17. Far away

To hold her hand's, way too far.
To see her eyes, it was way too far.
The smoke of kif.
Made my mind say, what if,
The reality was an illusion.
What if it's an delusion.
thinking of that.
Mind driven to madness.
Heart to sadness.
Hands to do badness.
The eyes, can't close,
Anxiety that glows,
like sun.
Hand's holding a gun.
Towards my head.
It's impossible, to see dead.

18. Emptiness

To hold on,
Need a pill,
Every night to fill,
her emptiness.
For a journey through past,
To taste life once again.
That's the place i wanna be,
To see her again,
To love her again.
To hold her again.
Mistakes i've done is a lot,
But still i try to fought.
But there was nothing,
Only an eternal void of emptiness

19. Trapped in hell

Gates between heaven and earth broke slightly,
by the strength of love.
Her kiss was a cure.
Her hands were my only shield.
Holding me tight.
To not to fall inside the fight.
Her soul touching mine.
To make my heart think i'm fine.
Holding my soul,
From leaving my body.
Because she know i'll never end up in heaven.

20. Void

No one knew how much empty,
A smile I wear to cover everything.
The torment, it was plenty.
Still in search of the soul ! lost.
But it was anguish I found.
Being with you went away so fast.
Now only a song of sorrow with a tremendous amount of sound,
Runs through my mind.
Life was filled with agony.
It's so high that nobody could withstand.
But he stood against it,
Knowing he could never get back what he lost.

21. Heaven in hell

Some souls are rare.
The thing i fell for is her hair.
Like a butterfly, my heart flies.
Just by looking into her eyes.
In her eyes mine got buried Under,
How to escape?, i wonder.
But inside the thunder,
I'm trapped.
Still it was paradise,
By her love,
By her touch,
I found a tiny heaven in that hell,
I was rotting.

22. Journey through pain

Pain comes to stay,
To run, There's no way.
Standing at a bay,
Of a sea filled with tears.
Pain eased, by her Smile.
But only for a while.
After that, started the sail,
Through the tears.
Holding her gift, Through the journey.
On that i sence Vellichor.
To the dead i Limerence.
Saw a Silhouette,
Walking towards that,
The way kept stretching.
Path was on fire,
Yet walking, For the love that i care.

23. Survivor

Drowned to the edge of anxiety.

Now only one border,

Left to emptiness.

Nobody could hear my screams.

Because it was all inside my dreams.

Can't explain the pain, It's extreme.

Shutting my mind to silence the screams.

Those violent screams has no words.

And it's hard to explain in herds.

No one could hear my mind,

And the cure, No one can find.

Giving me happiness for a moment & taking it from my hands.

Just to remind me again, That everything will turn into Sands,

Someday.

Making more painful,

Thought i was dying.

But rewinding every moments,

It really made me stronger,

A Survivor.

From that End, Another journey begins.

24. Love & drugs

Got friends with drugs.
To them i begs.
To cure my pain.
To ease my urge to cut the vein.
Need something to fill the void
But i never thought i'll be toyed,
By them.
They showed me path to escape the reality.
From this world which was full of brutality.
Love and drugs were same.
Because both were hard to tame.

25. Dimness

All hope of holding her hands shattered.
And after that nothing ever mattered.
Hid myself inside, In the illusion of ardent spirits.
In an eternal void of emptiness.
Eyes filled with dimness.
Can't see any hope.
Keeping myself busy,
Just to feel alright.
But every time i pause.
The pain it reignites.

26. Unfulfilled

Never wanted anything, But future,
With you.
But all i got was torture.
All i wanted was a better tomorrow.
But all i ended up with is sorrow.
She took away my youth,
When she left.
And reminded me once again the truth.
She came with a flower.
But that lasted only a hour.
The day i wanted to last,
Forever.
But went away so fast

27. My vow

Saw dark
Saw light
Once darkness was filled,
But her love made it change.
She guided me to an arcade,
Which faded,
All darkness.
Wanted to leave the past
And at last,
She made it possible.
True love won't desert Us,
Though we touched and,
Went on seperate ways,
You should know,
My vow
That i'll still love.
On your good and bad days,
Even if you are alive or not,
Even if you are in heaven or hell,
Even if it's impossible to touch.
My feelings will live as long as i.
And last as long as my,
Last breath.

28. Mentally dead

Watching rain falling gently,
Made my mind mentally,
Dead.
Each drop of rain,
Oozing every bit of pain,
Through my heart,
Ripping it apart.
Tried love.
Tried drugs.
If came a time to choose,
I'll say drug.
Both will kill,
But have to choose one to fill,
This emptiness.

29. You're mine & I'm yours

A million stars shining,
Still my eye were fixed on you.
She had a glow that,
Brighter than stars,
And beautiful than moon.
She took care of my broken heart,
And showed my soul how to fly.
She led me to tomorrow's light,
From these dark cold days.
Let me kiss you,
And show you what real love,
And bliss.
Come with me my dear,
It's time to leave the past behind,
She said.
Let's fly to a place were I'm yours,
And your mine.

30. Is this all you got god?

By that pain,
Yelling loudly in his mind,
Couldn't move his body,
Can't tell anyone,
Suffering silently.
How much pain,
Can a body withstand?
No one knew,
Until they suffered and lived,
Nobody can live,
After suffering that much.
But he lived,
With all those pain,
He stood up,
And said,
Is this all you got god?

31. Luna

Every Night watching the moon,
They asked, Why are you so obsessed with it.
And I said,
Moon reminded me of her.
Soo close that i can see,
But yet soo far.
The Moon reminded me of,
her bright beautiful eyes.
Which spread light,
To my life,
When it was filled with,
All dark thoughts and painful memories.
She came when i was Dying,
And made my heart blossom again.
Don't know when will the last day of us together.
Still enjoying every second of moments.
Enjoying as it's the last.

32. Stories of tears

You're not here anymore,
Last thing you gave was a kiss,
And that's what i miss,
The most.
Eyes filled with tears,
Fell.
Every drop has it's own story to tell,
My mind already knows.
But its my heart
That's not willing to,
Give up & forget.

33. Silent sufferers

Some are silent sufferers.
Wanted to reach out help.
But never found any cure.
Never found any care.
Memories were like bullet.
Some made me fear.
And some made my heart tear.
Showed me Hell,
Burning me Alive.
Darkness spreading like fire.
To see the slightest light I desire.

34. No faith left

Soul i wanted to find.
Both our heart i wanted to bind.
But God wasn't too kind,
To allow allow that.
Infront of him I sat.
Asking to give her back.
He said, if you can take her back,
Then try for yourself.
Born as a mortal,
Can't do the deed of an immortal.
Some fates are written in blood.
That can never be rewritten or changed.
This was our fate.
And there was no faith left.

35. On who given hope by love

She was a goddess that he couldn't touch,
But can feel,
The strong presence of love,
That he could see in her face.
Love that connected the two sides of the world.
A feeling that drove their minds mad.
Each moment passed as their love grew.
Both intending to hold each other.
But yet they couldn't.
Trying to reach her hands.
Trying to spread his wings,
To fly to her.
He did everything he could.
But still her hands had to wait yet another year.
But thoughts of her today,
Made him think,
He should've gone to her earlier.
An year has passed,
After she fled to heaven.
Yet every moment,
He can still feel her hands,
That he was unable to touch.
Wrapping around his body,
Like a blanket in winter,

She made him feel safe.
Made him feel he's not alone.
On her last days,
Her hands he couldn't hold.
For that,
Still her heart he holds.
Her untouched hands,
Holding his hands,
Every night.
To keep him from loosing the fight.

36. Happy memories

Sorrow was like the deofol.
Yet i tried to be a beadurinc.
Trying to survive i swincan.
But every time when i gather hope.
Misery once again onginnan.
Because of that,
To the living i forhtian.
All of her love,
All of her dreams.
All of that i alone dreogan.
Every moments was like andsaca.
Each memory only wanted amyrran.
But when i stood besides it,
I came to know that,
It was all just my happy memories.

37. Denied

Heavenly world was so dark and wide.
In that she hide.
To me, myself i chide.
To see her, it was denied.
Was in worst mental state,
And I can't no more wait.
My whole energy is spent,
By the immortal rules i tried to bent.

38. How can I be sober?

They're telling me to sober up.
But how can i ?.
To not to feel.
To not to die.
To not to fear.
I need these pills.
With or without this i'll die.
So i choose a way to fly,
From this world,
Without pain.

39. Heart aches

I'm still getting these heart aches.
Is it because of that person?
Or is it because of that feeling?
Her fingers crossed through mine,
For one last time.
Her eyes said adios,
But the feeling never left.
Feeling that kept me alive,
Was the one that ending my heart.
Never knew.
Until the death of soul.

40. Hoping for the rain of roses

In reality it's an end.
But still hopes ,
For a miracle.
In reality it's over.
But still heart shouting,
Maybe it'll be okay tomorrow.
wandering in the illusion,
Of darkness.
Hoping it's gonna rain Roses,
Someday.
But in reality,
The purple hyacinth was the one,
Felled all over him.

41. Monsters hiding inside

Don't know how to stop hearts aching.
All her smile , was faking.
To the eternal loop of fear, she's taking,
me.
Trusting you, i was mistaking.
To see the end of this loop i was waiting.
The physical body, they forsaking
A mind dead body, they making.
No path for escaping.
Monster in head, started shaping.

42. Still smiles & sings

Listening to music.

To ease the hurting.

Those who do not weep,

Do not see,

What's real elation.

In spite of tears,

In spite of fears,

In spite of pain,

In spite of all painfully sufferings,

Something within me,

Still smiles and sings.

43. Heart has to pay

Being sober since the day,
You left.
Because my heart has to Pay,
This much pain.
It made me think she was mine.
Me wanting more misery,
Wanting more sore.
Never wanted my heart to feel Relief,
Again.
Only wanted grief.
Because heart Should never Love again.

44. Light of my life

Her bright beautiful eyes,
Looking at me, in certain ways.
Her voice, like a melody,
Running through my ears.
That's the song I only could hear.
Her smile its can be compared,
To the stars in the skies.
And can get lost in her eyes.
Take my eyes out of her's,
Heart denies.

45. Teenage

Everything begins at a certain age.
Trapped inside this sorrowful stage.
She was sage,
But I'm stuck inside this cage.
Eyes showed sad.
Lost every tears i had.
Every pain was by love.
From all, it was above.
Mind was right,
Also heart.
Dark void spreading tonight.

46. Filled my sight

Was carrying the darkness of hundred nights,
In my eyes.
She filled my sight with a thousand moon.
That feeling was bright.
Then came the end of her time.
That again showed me the darkside.
And that time it was for eternity

47. My love never died

I know i'm gonna fail.
But still to heaven i set sail.
That gate i wanted to open.
With a heart that was broken.
Then a flicker of light came.
Woke up with knife in my hand.
To die, That was mind's stand.
The creator writes,
You both should never be on same sight.
I couldn't give her sunshine,
With the few little moment with her.
But my vow was never broken.
Stood beside her.
Even on the hardest rain.

48. Destined to be separated

She made me the happiest and saddest i ever been.
But we weren't destined to be together.
Because of all my sin.
There was no hope that we'll unite.
I said we'll stay together.
She said we'll stay together.
But never knew our hope will shatter this soon.
She loved and left.
I loved and now there's nothing left.
Destiny separated us between two worlds.
Heart started to burn.
Truth knowing that she could never return.

49. Endless

Head filled with endless buzzing.
Heart filled with endless scars,
And eyes that are drained.
That's how pain is.
Nobody could control that.
It comes when it wishes,
And goes when it done teaches.
Mind is shouting tremendously.
Heart filled with darkness.
All drowning me to sadness.
Every piece of hope shattered.
Thought i was sane.
Until the day wounds started to pain.
All that pain i kept it bottled.
And that's making me insane.

50. Until my day comes

Stuck inside the cage if misery.
Why do i have to suffer?
Why do i have to die,
A hundred times before the actual.?
Why do i alone suffer?
All started on the day you passed away.
You left in a midway.
Which left me in sorrow.
I choose to end this.
But what's the difference.
Still going to end up in hell,
And i know that well.
So i choose to stay,
In this cage of misery,
Until my day comes.
Till then there's no end to my numbs.

51. Torment

Always checks under my bed,
To see if there's any dead.
Always thought monsters were under my bed.
But never knew it's hiding inside my head.
When the day time started to torment the soul.
All the monsters inside woke up.
And started to eat from the inside.
Mind started to scream.
Heart started to bleed.
Last hope was to end.
But because of the promise,
I tried to stay.
Even though my heart was bleeding.
Even though my mind was pleading
I withstood.
To the death i said,
No matter how much agony.
No matter how much misery.
No matter how much suffering.
I will forever keep my vow.

52. Every sin has a price to pay

For all his sin.
She was the price he paid.
Her soul left this world.
But his stayed.
To the god he begs.
Take us both,
Or spare us both.
That was the oath,
We both took.
Dreamt of togetherness.
Broke and turned into sadness.
Now stuck inside a loop of fearfulness.
Without a hope of escape.

53. Aleena

Crossed my life a girl.
With voice as divine as an angel.
She was pearl.
Who sang to god in heaven.
She singing,
Is a sound in comparison with a soft droplets of rain,
Falling gently,
On my heart.
Running through my veins,
To my darkest part of soul,
And sprouted a blaze of bliss.
Voice which flooded me with pleasure,
Which pierced me like a sword.
Your sweet song in my ear,
Is what i crave the most,
More than the air i breathe.
Her voice,
Made me feel like i was in a magical place.

54. Lost all reasons left to stay alive

For me every night is war,
And every day preparing for it.
Light to escape is way to far.
I don't know what to do anymore.
They Broke my heart,
And called me heartless.
My life was like an art,
Which filled with misery.
Tears, the river of soul,
Flooded through my eyes.
Slowly loosing reasons to stay.
Can't go through it yet another day.

55. Ache has no end

A boy trapped in a place,
Which created by his agony.
Thought of escaping it.
But how can someone outrun their mind.
Tears i can wipe.
Ache will stay.
Oh soul be ready for something worse.
Because i know it's a curse.

56. One who made me love myself

Some souls suffer silently.
With voices in head so violently.
Yes i lost you,
But there's a slight view,
From hell to heaven.
So I could see you.
I never lost my love for you,
Even though i lost you.
You came to me at a worst time,
When i truthfully hated who i was,
And who i will be.
But you gaved me your love,
And by that,
You made me love myself.

57. Fake hope

Her eyes were like a sea,
Which made me see only love in it.
Her eyes were like magnet,
Which attracted my soul,
Kept me intacted with her like a fool.
Then i saw thousands of waves,
In her eyes again,
Waves filled with pain and lie.
That made me cry.
i Want to die,
Just to end this pain

58. Her words

Day was like nightmare,
And night was like hell.
Moon was my friend,
And rain was my comfort.
Want to sleep like i'm in heaven.
But when the eye closes.
All i see are death.
Understood happiness was an illusion.
And emptiness is reality.
Life was hell.
Which was full,
Of dead faces and flowers.
Want to cry.
But my eyes were dry.
All endings are new beginning,
So let go and trust,
She said,
But how can i?
Before this every time, it was we.
Now the only one who left here was me.
Stuck between don't wanna go back,
And couldn't go forward.

59. No amount of courage is enough to die

A room with dim blinking light,
With smoke in my hand,
With music in my ears.
Going through all painful moments,
In a blink of an eye.
Experiencing every pain,
All at once.
With a mind dead body,
Trying to kill himself.
Trying pills.
Trying drugs.
With a knife.
With a blade.
But nothing brought courage,
To end this damaged soul.
And now making a everyone a fool,
By the smile i wear.

60. Slow death

Getting those anxiety waves again
Mastering the art of letting go,
Infront of all those memories I bow.
Each memories piercing a sword,
With all of those words ,
From the past.
Not intending to kill me fast.
Slowly, slowly,
Slowly entering my heart,
And made it stop.

61. Wanted to heal

Wanted the truth,
Wanted to move forth.
Some drugs I buy,
Trying to die.
Because I wanted to heal.
Because I wanted to feel.
Without that the only option is to kill.
Because all dark thoughts was filled,
Inside my mind,
But also I wanted to bind,
My soul and heart.
But I couldn't.

62. Not every smile is friend

Came to heal themself.
Gone after they are healed.
They came for their pain.
They came for their gain.
Thought everyone was sane.
End, the heart broken was mine.
Thought every smile was friend.
Thought every word was friend.
But behind everyone's smile,
Was filled with vile,
Which was a huge pile,
Of negative thoughts and darkness.

63. Was there no truth?

Her charming smile and short hair.
The loses how can I bear?.
Fear turned into pain.
Who would've knew this would've happen.
We had a love so pure.
A disease nobody can't cure.
Was there no truth?
Our hearts were connected.
Soon after there was nothing but darkness.
There was nothing but weakness.
Ended up in utter sadness.

64. My struggle to escape

Eternal Amount of quiteness.
There was nothing to express.
Pain flowing in a same rhyme,
Without giving any time.
Why God loth?.
Why is he not giving up anything?.
In pain, us both
Struggling to escape.

65. End of her story

Going through the worst days.
Death I sees,
Every minute.
Her face I sees every second.
To my mind came every moment.
Crying to death,
And moving forth,
Was an impossible thing.
A bell from an unknown place rings.
God opened his wings,
Flying to earth,
Came saying that it's the end of her birth.
Crying.
Begging.
But what can I do?.
I can't fly behind him,
No mortal can.
Excepted that iam alone,
And cursed god.

66. The day my first love was born

Waiting under the shade of a tree.
To the rain to ease.
Holding her hands,
Feeling her breath.
With the drops of rain,
Everyone was shivering with the cold.
But I was warm,
My mind was warm.
She holding my hands,
Standing close infront of me,
Made my heart stop for a moment.
I couldn't look at her eyes,
Because it was the one,
That's making my heart stop.
That was the moment,
I felled in love with her.

67. Pain has no death

All the way, I lost.
With hurting at its most.
Mind said,
There's a way,
To end all of this
Wanted end this,
But the way could,
Hurts some people.
To end this pain,
By doing that,
My pain will be given to another person.
My body can die,
But still that pain will live through her.
I can withstand this.

68. All those noises

Sitting alone in my room,
Don't wanna go out,
Others arguing outside,
Me in my room,
Covering my ears,
With fears,
In my eyes.
This fear ends,
When the fight ends.

69. Fallen angel

Unmatured days where more happiest.
Because we where least saddest.
Remembering those days,
Inside my room,
At a rainy night,
With smoke all over,
Crying inside.
Slight tear from left eye fell,
With a small smile,
He went into the past.
When i was falling,
I never saw any hands behind me.
Fell from sky,
To the ground,
And people called him,
The fallen angel.
With wings teared apart,
He couldn't fly back,
To where he came from.
And lived his immortal life,
In this mortal world,
With only pain.

70. Her presence was enough

Like a see all pains form.
And was going through storm.
To ease this, I have to be tough,
And her presence was enough.
She cured my heart,
Without a single word.
She standing besides me,
Was way enough than any words.

71. Fight to death

A boy who was afraid of nights,
Because of all those fights,
Every night is a fight to death,
Not with swords,
Not with guns,
Not with god,
And not with satan.
It was him fighting himself,
A fight fought by minds,
A fight fought by darkness and light.
With all that war,
He realised that it was soo far,
From the light.

Every End Is A New Beginning

T0 every pain there will come a day that they will die or its gonna make you strong.

Remember that no matter how hard the walk is, the end will be paradise. Don't stop because its hurting.

www.ingramcontent.com/pod-product-compliance
Lightning Source LLC
Chambersburg PA
CBHW021126130726
47988CB00003B/1188